BISHOP~
and the lost
TIDE M. ~

Tide Mills in 1853 from the southeast, showing part of the village.

David Lyndhurst

S.B. Publications

To the late Neal Thompson, good friend
and one-time resident of Tide Mills

First published in 2001 by S B Publications,
14 Bishopstone Road, East Sussex, BN25 2UB

Revised and reprinted 2008

ISBN 978-185770-334-4

Layout by Vital Signs Publishing
Email: *info@vitalsignspublishing.co.uk*

CONTENTS

ACKNOWLEDGMENTS

My grateful thanks to the late 'Mac' McCarthy who, before his death in 1993, gave permission to SB Publications to reproduce information and illustrations from his book *Sussex River, Seaford to Newhaven*; also to Dr Martin Bell for his permission to reproduce parts of his report *Excavations At Bishopstone*, Luke Barber, Anne Fontaine, Paul Haynes, Marilyn Higson of the Ironbridge Gorge Museum, Beverley Lyndhurst, Dr Gabor Thomas, Mr K Whitehead of the British Rail Property Board, the staffs of the East Sussex County Council Records Office and the Eastbourne Reference Library. The interpretation boards were installed at Tide Mills in 2004 as part of a partnership project between Sussex Probation Service and English Heritage Outreach to increase public access to the site.

Front Cover: *Tide Mills, Bishopstone, c. 1850. Reproduced with permission from the family of the artist, the late Stuart Broadhurst.*

The excavation site on the flat crest of Rookery Hill.

This 30 to 40 year-old Iron Age male with only six serviceable teeth in his jaws was buried in a storage pit on the edge of the settlement.

1

Rookery Hill, Bishopstone

Rookery Hill lies about two miles east of the present mouth of the river Ouse at Newhaven. It is a south-facing spur, rising to 50 metres, on the slope of the South Downs and the crest commands a view over Seaford Bay and the English Channel. The hill would in the past have formed a promontory of land, with the waters of the Ouse estuary on the western side and, on the eastern side, another stretch of water reaching almost to Bishopstone church. It was an ideal defensive position and was probably used as such from the late Iron Age up to the time of the Napoleonic Wars.

The top of the hill is flat. The eastern side ends abruptly in a steep slope, much overgrown, which drops down to the former estuary and the present village of Bishopstone. One can stand on the upper slopes and look down at the tree tops where the rooks nest, for the western slope drops less steeply on to land where many Mesolithic flints have been found. Further Mesolithic material has been discovered on Hawth Hill, which lies a mile to the south-east and would, in that period, have also had water on three sides.

There is little trace on the surface of Rookery Hill of its long history of settlements. Along the top of the spur on the western side there are eight round barrows of probable Bronze Age date. The only other obvious feature is a sizable terrace on the southern slope. However, in the course of excavating the foundations for the bungalows being built in 1967 on what was to become the Harbour View Estate, workmen uncovered a group of skeletons. The discovery was at once reported to the Sussex Archaeological Society and an extensive excavation of the site began under the direction of David Thomson. The soil was stripped off and a pagan Saxon cemetery revealed. Early in 1969 Martin Bell took over responsibility for the excavations and for further work carried out between 1970 and 1972 and again in 1974/5. More than a hundred fifth century Saxon graves were examined, the earliest in the group of Bronze Age barrows from which the cemetery had spread. Adjoining farmland was also excavated and traces of a number of Anglo-Saxon buildings were found, together with an earlier Iron Age and Romano-British settlement. The fields themselves appear to have been cultivated intermittently from Neolithic times.

When the Anglo Saxon settlement was abandoned – or did it perhaps just move to a lower level and became Bishopstone? – there was no more long-term occupation of Rookery Hill until the housing development of recent years. The discovery of a 4lb cannon ball of Armada date and a George III coin, dated 1797, in the lower part of a field near the Saxon cemetery, together with some tiles and other materials which can be dated to the Napoleonic Wars, suggest that in the intervening centuries it was used occasionally for defensive purposes.

Among the metal objects found was this bronze brooch of a type last used in Britain in AD 70.

A Romano-British handle, or toggle, of sheep bone with carved decoration was found on the site.

6

2

Bishopstone Village

There was a settlement in the valley below Rookery Hill as early as the tenth century and in the green areas to the west and south of the church, banks and ditches can clearly be seen. After the Norman Conquest Bishopstone became part of the Rape of Pevensey, the honour of which passed to the L'Aigle or Aquila family after the treachery of the Count of Mortain in 1101, when Henry I's army was waiting outside Pevensey Castle for the invading forces of Robert, Duke of Normandy.

The Domesday Book of 1068 records that in Flexborough Hundred:

> *The Bishop of Chichester holds BISHOPSTONE in lordship.*
> *Before 1066 it answered for 25 hides; now the same . . .*
> *30 villagers with 9 smallholders have 30 ploughs.*
> *Meadow, 40 acres; woodland, 3 pigs from pasturage;*
> *from grazing, 1 pig in 3.*
> *Value before 1066 £26; later £11; now £20 . . .*

The bishops of Chichester held land in both West and East Sussex, including a fair amount around Lewes. Bishopstone, the manor of which included parts of Norton, Denton and Heathfield, was their major holding in the Lewes area and they had an official residence there, on a site a few yards south of the churchyard. It was in this mansion, over the weekend of 31 August to 2 September 1324, that Bishop John de Langton entertained Edward II and his entourage on his only visit to Sussex as king. As Prince of Wales he had been a frequent visitor to to the county, particularly to Ditchling where he kept the stud of horses his father had given him in 1304.

The windmill at Bishopstone, which belonged in 1189 to 'Pagan, the clerk,

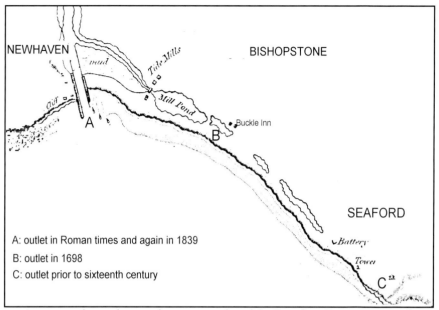

A conjectural map showing the various outlets of the Ouse from Roman times to the present day.

The following labels appear on the map:

NEWHAVEN

BISHOPSTONE

SEAFORD

Buckle Inn

A: outlet in Roman times and again in 1839
B: outlet in 1698
C: outlet prior to sixteenth century

The old Buckle Inn was demolished in 1964 and a new one built beside it at a cost of some £28,000. That also has gone and now, on the site opposite the sailing club, there is a private house.

of good memory', was bought from his heir, Reynold de London, by Bishop Seffrid II for five marks (£6.33p). He left it in trust to the canons of Chichester cathedral to pay for a Mass to be said for his soul on the anniversary of his death, stipulating the exact amount each of the participating clerics should receive. If any of the canons were not present, eightpence (3p) of the shilling (5p) they would have received was to go to the poor.

Until towards the end of the sixteenth century the course of the Ouse ran parallel to the present coastline from Meeching to Seaford and the river entered the English Channel under Seaford Head. There was a ferry crossing on the road from Bishopstone to Seaford, near the site of the old Buckle Inn, and the road then continued along the spit of land on the seaward side of the river – on much the same line as it takes today. In the fourteenth century the ferry was operated by 'Richard Beselin atte Botte' who, in return for conveying across the river 'the Bishop and his four carriages and men in his service and all avers (other goods or farm beasts) coming from Bishopstone Manor', was allowed to graze twenty-five ewes and one ram with the manor flocks and receive food for himself and one other.

Some time around 1567 the Ouse burst through the shingle bank to form a new mouth between the present site of Tide Mills and the site of the Buckle Inn. The entrance to the Cinque Port of Seaford soon silted up and the haven became landlocked. Bishopstone found itself with an area of water between the church and Rookery Hill – where there is still a pond to this day – which formed a natural harbour. It prospered for some 200 years and in 1698 it was the home port of at least nine vessels, some of them quite large. However, in a storm in the 1750s the river broke through to the sea by Meeching, thus creating a 'New Haven' there and leaving the harbour at Bishopstone to suffer the same fate as the one at Seaford.

In the reign of Henry VIII (1509-1547), the land comprising the manor of Bishopstone was leased to the Pelham family, thus establishing a link that was to last for 300 years. Early Pelhams served as knights under the Aquilas from soon after the Norman Conquest and one was Constable of Pevensey Castle under Henry IV and Treasurer of England.

During the battle of Poitiers in 1356 Sir John de Pelham captured the King of France. One story goes that he seized the French king by one of the buckles on his armour, another version is that the king's sword got caught in Pelham's buckle. Whatever the cause, the buckles were added to the Pelham arms, some say as an augmentation of honour for the capture of the French king – others that they were added in the seventeenth century by a Herald interested in history.

The first Pelham to be connected with the manor of Bishopstone was probably Sir Nicholas who, in 1545, saved Seaford from an attack by the French fleet which had put in to the bay after unsuccessful raids on Brighthelmstone and Meeching. He rallied the inhabitants and led them against the invaders, who retreated back to their ships leaving some hundred corpses on the beach in an area known to this day as the Buckle.

The Pelham coat of arms.

Sir John Pelham, the third baronet, was a huntmaster to King Charles II and in 1663 was commissioned by James Compton, Earl of Northampton and Master of the Leash, to be his deputy for a district ten miles around Bishopstone with authority to 'take so many greyhounds as he may think convenient for His Majesty's sport, and to seize other dogs which may be offensive to same.'

However, it was Thomas Pelham-Holles, created Duke of Newcastle by George I in 1715, who made the greatest impression on the lives of the inhabitants of the manor of Bishopstone, which he inherited with the rest of the vast estates of the Pelhams from his uncle in 1711. It was he who, in 1761, on his second term as Prime Minister, secured the passage through Parliament of an Act for the construction of a water mill to be driven by the tides on the coast to the east of Newhaven. Another feature of the landscape for which he was responsible was a plantation of trees, mostly beeches, at the foot of Rookery Hill. Unlike the tide mill it is still there today and it is still known as Duke's Walk.

His political influence in the area was unchallenged. Seaford became his pocket borough and the candidates he favoured won every election from 1717 until his death in 1768. He secured William Pitt the Elder's election in 1747 by giving an eve-of-poll party for the local gentry and influential farmers at Bishopstone Place. It lasted until daybreak when the revellers were bundled into carriages and taken to the town hall to vote. The Duke sat next to the returning officer and stared intently at every voter – and erstwhile guest – who appeared in front of him. Few dared, in the circumstances, to vote against the Whig interest.

Thomas Pelham-Holles died childless and Baron Pelham of Stanmer, created first Earl of Chichester in 1801, inherited the bulk of the Pelham estates, which spread over eleven counties. Bishopstone Place, built originally as a hunting lodge on the site of the original mansion, which had been used and improved by successive lords of the manor, was put up for sale or to let in 1772. Neither buyer nor tenant could be found and it was demolished in 1831. Many of the blue-glazed bricks of which it was built were salvaged by the inhabitants and found their way into the walls of later buildings in the village.

Today, all that is left of Bishopstone Place is some of its extensive underground cellarage. During the Second World War the cellars were used as an air raid shelter but the entrance is now very much overgrown and two passages from them leading under the churchyard have been blocked off.

On this card of Bishopstone, posted in 1936, the correspondent writes: 'Did Brighton yesterday but not struck and county between definitely spoilt. Bishopstone is now threatened by at least two huge building estates . . .'

11

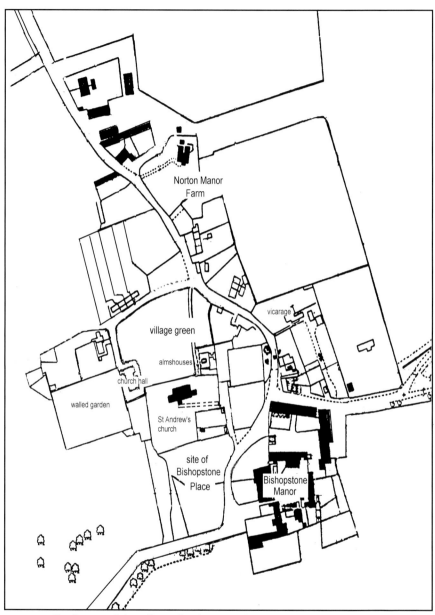

Norton Manor
Farm

vicarage

village green

almshouses

church hall

walled garden

St Andrew's
church

site of
Bishopstone
Place

Bishopstone
Manor

Sketch map of the village of Bishopstone showing the features mentioned in the text.

Across the road from the site is a house that was built by Baron Pelham in 1688 for his agent. By 1835 it had been enlarged and given the name Bishopstone Manor. It was occupied for eighty years by the Farncombes, a family that leased Bishopstone Manor Farm, one of the two large farms in the parish – the other was Norton – that came into being in the 1770s when the majority of the agricultural tenancies of the estate were being changed, as they became vacant, from copyhold to leasehold. The Farncombes were succeeded by the Willetts at the farm and then Bishopstone Manor became a kindergarten school for girls for a few years until, in 1939, it was taken over by the Army and a unit of French Canadians was billeted there. After the war it was a guesthouse but the enterprise was unsuccessful and in 1952 it was converted into three semi-detached properties now known as Bishopstone Manor North, West and South. There is a plaque on the middle portion with the inscription 'T.P. 1688' and the buckle, from the Pelham family coat-of-arms, which appears on Pelham properties throughout Sussex.

The village green to the north of the church appears on a Pelham estate map as the Hagg and is known locally as the Egg – but for what reason no one can say. The two pieces of land it comprises were registered as a village green separately by East Sussex County Council in 1968 but its Register of Common Land and Village Greens was destroyed in an office fire in 1993. Another feature over which there is a question mark is the square of land surrounded by a high brick wall immediately to the west of the church hall – which was the village school from 1849 until it closed in 1944. It does not appear on the Pelham estates map of Bishopstone of 1732 but it is on the 1777 estate map as a 'new garden'. Later Ordnance Survey maps show trees within the square but these had disappeared by the 1960s and been replaced by a tennis court. Around this time, villagers recollect, the square also accommodated John Willett's herd of deer. Today the walls enclose only unkempt grass.

Bishopstone House was built in 1844 as a vicarage and was used as such until the 1930s when it became a private house. For many years it was owned by the author, Dennis Mackail, brother of novelist Angela Thirkell. Their mother was the only daughter of Pre-Raphaelite painter Sir Edward Burne-Jones and through her they were related to two other famous Rottingdean residents, Rudyard Kipling and Stanley Baldwin, Prime Minister at the time of Edward VIII's abdication.

Dennis Mackail was a stage designer before *What Next?*, a light but literary novel that he wrote in five weeks, which was a runaway success. He followed it up with a book a year but, unlike his sister, whose books on the lives and loves of top-drawer families in their country houses retain a devoted following, he is rarely read nowadays.

Barrack Cottages, which have been converted to a private house, were built to accommodate troops in the Napoleonic Wars. Further along the road is Norton. This small hamlet within the parish of Bishopstone obviously derived its name from its geographical position within the parish – it is at the northern corner. Here at The Cottage, now called Norton House, James Hurdis, one-time vicar of Bishopstone and Professor of Poetry at Oxford, was born in 1763 and lived at intervals with his mother and sisters until his death in 1801. His last and longest poem, *The Favourite Village*, was written in 1800 and he set up the type and printed it himself on the press he had at The Cottage.

There are memorials to him in the church at Bishopstone, one erected by his sisters and another from his friend and fellow poet, William Hayley. It begins:

Hurdis! Ingenious Poet and Divine!
A tender sanctity of thought was thine

A close-up of one of the carved heads.

Bishopstone's Church of St Andrew is one of the oldest in Sussex, dating as it does from the eighth century. The tower has four recessed stages, each one divided from the next by a string course. It is 45 feet to the corbel table, beneath which, on each side of the tower, is a row of carved heads, now much eroded by weathering, with a pyramidal spire above. In the middle of the second stage on the north wall of the tower, above a narrow window, is a single carved head.

The church's south porch is pre-Conquest. It was originally a porticus, a feature of Saxon churches usually built on to the south or north face to provide some space for private prayer, burials or Masses, and it was converted into the porch in the twelfth

14

century. Above it is a sundial with the name EADRIC inscribed within a Greek fret border. Opinions vary as to whether the name refers to the stonemason whose work it is or to the Eadric who, say the Anglo Saxon Chronicles, was made an ealdorman of Mercia in 1007.

The outer doorway is a typical example of eleventh and twelfth century Norman doorways and has shafts with carved capitals and chevron ornament on its rounded arch. Renovations of the righthand quoin of the porch are easily distinguishable. The work was done in the 1980s and at the same time a new gnomon was mounted on the sundial. This is slightly off-centre because of the difficulty of removing the remains of the old gnomon without causing any damage to the main structure.

The entrance to the tower, the roof of which was re-shingled with oak in 1954, is from the western end of the nave through a rounded arch. In the west wall, in addition to a high circular light, are two single-splayed windows, one above the other, the upper one being very small and the lower one paned with stained glass depicting Saint Luke.

The belfry contains two bells, a treble and a tenor, contained in an S-type frame. They were cast by Lester and Pack in 1761. Previously there were three, 'in 1724, all cracked' says George P Elphick in *Sussex Bells and Belfries*.

The sun dial with its new gnomon.

Until the mid-eighteenth century churches had a choir to lead the singing, often from a specially erected gallery at the west end of the church. Some choirs later evolved into choir bands, playing instruments such as violins, flutes, clarinets and bassoons. A change in ecclesiastical policy in the 1850s resulted in the abolition of choir bands, the removal of their galleries and the installation of organs. The gallery of St Andrew's church was removed in 1848 and a barrel organ installed. In 1896 this was removed and replaced by the present organ, which is on the north side of the choir and has seventeen metal pipes and thirteen wooden ones open to view. It was restored and re-voiced in 1916 by the firm of Cartwright and Son and further renovated in the 1950s.

15

The font is of twelfth century date and, like most early fonts, is made of a hard freshwater Chara limestone. This stone is found at Purbeck and on the Isle of Wight and was probably transported by sea to coastal areas of the mainland. The font cover is heavy, made of carved oak, and was presented to the church by Fanny Cooper, a member of the family who originally leased and then bought Norton Farm from the Pelhams.

The nave arcade has a single rounded pier and semi-circular half-piers attached to the walls, all with moulded capitals, and in the south wall there are narrow pointed-arch windows. Set in the wall at the east end of the north aisle is a small, stained glass window depicting St Andrew. The north and south walls of the chancel have two blank arches each, one capital scalloped. The arches have zigzag or chevron ornament to the east and plain roll moulding to the west. There are six fine stained glass windows in the south wall, four showing biblical scenes and the other two patterned. On a sunny day the coloured effect in the light thrown on to the altar is delightful. High up in the east wall are two round windows. There is also a stained glass window in the sanctuary, centrally above the altar, depicting the Ascension. It was installed in memory of Bishopstone Manor tenant farmer, George Farncombe, who died on 25 September 1858.

The carvings on the firestone slab.

The sanctuary rib vaulting was done when the church was restored by the Earl of Chichester in 1849, very probably by the builders responsible for similar vaulting in Icklesham church. While this work was in progress a 4ft 2½inch (1.283m) monumental slab was found set in the wall to form a lintel above a fireplace at the end of a pew. Carved on it, within three circles of intertwined rope, were two doves drinking from a tall vase, the Agnus Dei, and, at the base, a Calvary cross. This slab, which is of firestone, was removed and set into the floor of the new vestry. In 1885 it was transferred to the south wall of the tower. The eastern arch of the sanctuary is triple-shafted with multi-scalloped capitals. It is pointed with a hood moulding of dogtooth and has a carved face mounted

16

St Andrew's church. The Catt family tomb is in the left foreground.

over the apex. The arch to the west is of Early English re-doing with stiff-leaf capitals and fine mouldings.

In the churchyard is the Catt family vault in which are buried a former owner of the tide mill, William Catt, who died on 4 March 1853, aged seventy-three; his wife Hannah, who was forty-six when she died on 13 January 1823; his daughter, Mary Ann, who died on 16 February 1826, aged eighteen; his son Edgar, who died on 15 June 1832, aged thirteen; and his daughter Elizabeth Willett who died on 4 April 1863 aged sixty-six. There are memorial tablets to the Catt family inside the church as well and the almshouses at the south east corner of the village green were endowed by George Catt in memory of his first wife, Mary Anne, née Cooper, who died at the age of twenty-nine on 15 April 1856.

A more recent monument in the churchyard is a memorial, in the form of a sundial, to the memory of Cecilia, wife of the Reverend W J Squirrell, Vicar of Bishopstone from 1936 to 1945.

Internal and external restoration of Bishopstone church was completed in 2006. Interior walls were stripped of render, revealing interesting aspects, including Saxon stonework comparable to that of the earliest churches in the country.

The remains of three previously blocked-up windows, one Saxon in the north-west wall of the nave and two others visible high in the east side of the tower wall, were revealed, and on the west wall of the nave was discovered a small area of medieval chevron-style painting on original lime-wash.

In the sanctuary, traces of a piscina (stone water basin) and an imposing aumbry (recess in a wall for sacramental vessels) were also uncovered.

Uncovering Bishopstone's Anglo-Saxon Past

Archaeological excavations led by Dr Gabor Thomas on behalf of the University of Kent and the Sussex Archaeological Society between 2002 and 2005 unearthed a wealth of new information on the origins of Bishoptone village. Discoveries on the village green confirmed that during the three centuries leading up until the Norman conquest (otherwise known as the Late Anglo-Saxon period) the church was surrounded by a dense swathe of rectangular timber houses and other ancillary buidlings, some indicative of high status. Typically for the period, the houses were rectangular in plan and constructed of timber posts set into the foundation trenches with wattle-and-daub providing walling; roofs were most likely thatched.

Excavation revealed that some of the twenty or so unearthed structures encroached upon the outer limits of an earlier Christian cemetery, represented by forty graves from a mixed population of adults and children. Some of the adults showed signs of osteoarthritis and secondary bone disease relating to acute infection. Scientific dating indicates that this part of the early burial ground went out of use at some point during the 10th century, when the northern boundary of the churchyard was pulled back to its current alignment; this explains why Late Saxon timber buildings were superimposed on earlier graves.

At the time of writing, the current hypothesis is that the excavated remains belong to a manorial residence owned by the Bishops of Selsey (who held Bishopstone manor from the 9th century) or, more likely, one of their bailiffs. Artefacts recovered from the excavations show that in addition to acting as a private residence, the settlement was also functioning as a centre of craft production, with pottery and textile manufacture, as well as smithing and copper-alloy metalworking, all in evidence. A highlight of the excavation was the discovery of a smith's hoard containing a mixture of agricultural tools, locks and other structural fittings - one of the finest assemblages of ironwork from Late Anglo-Saxon England. The recovery of large quantities of animal bone, shell and other 'environmental' remains show that the community's dietary needs were met by a mixed regime of crop production and animal husbandry, supplemented by fish and shellfish recovered from the sea and surrounding salt-marsh.

The final definitive report on the findings was due to be published in late 2008 as a Council for British Archaeology research report. The excavations took place with the kind permission of landowner, Mr John Willett.

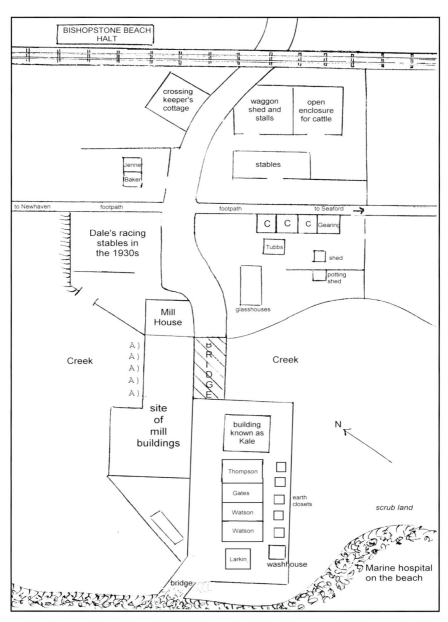

Sketch map of the village of Tide Mills in the 1900s before it was 'lost' as a result of 'sanitary defects' in 1936 and then, in 1939, to 'the exigencies of war'.

3

Tide Mills, Bishopstone

At the end of the seventeenth century the main exit to the sea for the River Ouse was near the present site of what was the village of Tide Mills and the whole area was a mixture of marshland and shingle. In 1735 a cut was made in the shingle bank below Castle Hill, Newhaven to allow the river once again to flow into the sea at the same place that it had done in Roman times. There was still a tidal flow through a subsidiary channel off the main river and barges were able to use this route behind the shingle bank at spring tides to bring goods from Newhaven harbour to the wharf near the Buckle Inn at the bottom of Hawth Hill, Bishopstone.

Somehow the potential of the area between the harbour mouth and the Buckle came to the notice of three West Sussex corn merchants, William Woods and John Challen of Chichester and John Woods of Chilgrove, who were seeking to expand their coastwise trade. They approached the lord of the manor, Thomas Pelham-Holles, Duke of Newcastle, and put to him their plan to build a flour-producing mill, which could be driven by the force of the tides coming into the mile-long creek that had previously formed part of the main river.

In 1761 the Duke granted the three merchants a 500-year lease of the creek and secured a private Act of Parliament for the construction across it of a dam for the mill. The Act, which also had the effect of forestalling any opposition to the closing of navigation at the eastern end of the creek, sets out the boundaries of the land on which the lessees proposed to:

> . . . *build, set up and erect one or more mill or mills in or upon the said creek or channel for grinding of corn and making or manufacturing the same into*

The tide mill from the west showing the five arches through which water flowed and, below, a drawing of the mill by J E Martin from an unsigned oil painting c1835.

flour, as well for home consumption as for exportation and for that purpose to make and build a weir dam or fender across the said channel or creek with proper floodgates or sluices therein to be opened with the flux and shut with the reflux of the tide; and thereby to collect and reserve a sufficient head or quantity of water for working the said mill during the time of such reflux. And they also propose to make a commodious wharf or quay at or near the said mill for loading and unloading corn meal and goods, and a convenient road to and from the same.'

It goes on to list the benefits that will accrue from the project:

'It is apprehended that the erecting and building of such mills, will not only facilitate the sale and disposition of the produce of the lands there but also render the navigation of the channel more practical and effectual and will consequently be of great benefit and advantage to the said country, and of publick utility.'

The structure, of typical Sussex boulder walling, was completed in 1768. There was also a house, a warehouse, which presumably served as a granary, and a coal wharf that could be reached by vessels of up to 140 tons. The mill, with its five pairs of millstones capable of grinding an average of 1,200 sacks of flour a week, stood on a five-arched dam across the creek. The arches housed the water-wheels, which were about 15 feet in diameter and undershot. They were driven by water released from the eastern millponds through the arches as the tide began to ebb. To the south of the mill was a sluice in the dam through which, on an incoming tide, water flowed into the millponds in the east. The mill was probably in use for about four to six hours during each tide.

The tidal channel to the west acted as a source of water for storing in the ponds and also provided access to the mill for shipping.

On 19 September 1791 the mill was advertised for sale in the *Sussex Weekly Advertiser*. It was described as 'a capital new Tide corn mill'. The asking price was £3,000 and it was bought by former Lamberhurst miller Thomas Barton who insured it with the Sun Life Insurance Company for £4,000. In 1795 Barton entered into a partnership with Edmund Catt but in 1801 he left and was succeeded by Edmund Catt's cousin, William Catt, who was in his early twenties and had run a small mill in Lamberhurst for the two previous years. William was the son of John Catt, a small farmer who had married into the Willett family.

William Catt was born in 1776 and was educated at a dame school. It is said that he showed little enthusiasm for book-learning but was fond of cricket. At the age of twenty-one he married Hannah Dawes from Ewhurst and they had twelve children, several of whom, in later life, adopted their grandmother's maiden name of Willett.

Edmund and William Catt increased the number of millstones at the mill from five to sixteen. In 1808 William bought out Edmund with financial assistance from two wealthy farmers, Edmund Cooper of Norton Farm and Thomas Farncombe of Bishopstone Farm. Catt and Cooper formed a partnership and in 1826 the company became William Catt and Sons, by which time much of the marshland had been drained and the mill operation had been greatly expanded.

As the mill thrived, a village with a population of about 100 grew up beside it to accommodate the mill workers whose hours were dictated by the tides. Flint cottages, some with lattice-work porches, were built for them and schooling was provided for their children.

Catt was a hard-headed business man with a strong personality and his word was law in the village. He regulated the time his workers returned home from the Buckle Inn of an evening by making sure that the three entrance gates

The village street of Tide Mills with workers' cottages facing the mill buildings against which are the espaliered pear trees in full leaf.

The rail head to Tide Mills showing part of the windmill on top of the granary.

to Tide Mills were firmly locked at 10.10pm. There was a cinder path along the coastline from Seaford, and Catt would lie in wait for latecomers in the twitten where it entered the village. On one occasion he caught two of his workmen climbing over the gate at 10.20pm, just ten minutes late, and withdrew all their privileges and confined them to the village for a month.

Tyrant he may have been, but his workers loved him – or at least one did. During a harvest supper one of his employees seized Catt by the hand saying: 'Give us yer hand sir. I love ye, I love ye, sir, but I'm damned if I bea'nt afeard of ye though'.

Catt enlarged the mill, increased the number of buildings for storage, added a blacksmith's and a carpenter's shop and an office building. A granary was built and above it a six-sided smock mill winded by a fantail and driven by patent sweeps was erected to drive hoisting gear. The eastern mill pond was enlarged and given a bigger sluice with a bridge over it which allowed access to the beach. The old channel on the east side of the mill was embanked and converted into a mill pond, water entering it from the creek at high tide through a lock on the west side of the pond. This increased the time the mill could operate as when the western pond began to empty, a sluice was opened and extra water was supplied from the eastern pond.

25

With the mill as a foundation, Catt built up a thriving business. During the Napoleonic Wars, he contracted to supply bread, flour and meat to the Army. Horse-drawn wagons regularly left Tide Mills bound for Portsmouth to supply the king's troops stationed in the Southern Counties and commanded by the Duke of Wellington.

Catt was also active in the development of coastal and riverside trade in grains, using the advantages of the mill site. He imported grain from France and, in partnership with William Cole, who owned a wharf in the harbour at Newhaven, he built up a local trade in flour and grain. His expertise was much in demand and in 1846 he was invited to the Chateau d'Eu to advise King Louis-Philippe on milling in France. He was able to return the compliment two years later when the French king was forced to abdicate and flee to England with his queen. The couple, both of them heavily disguised, landed at Newhaven with a few personal attendants and were taken to the Bridge Inn. According to the *Sussex County Magazine* of January 1937 and letters in later issues of that year, when the news of their arrival reached William Catt, he went at once to the

This engraving was originally published in the Sussex Weekly Advertiser, *the editor of which, William Lee, interviewed the exiled royals at the Bridge Hotel. Are the two young women behind the French king and queen Elizabeth and Caroline Catt and could the bearded man be their father, William?*

inn, accompanied by his two daughters, Elizabeth and Caroline, who waited on the royal couple as they breakfasted at the hotel.

Catt offered Louis-Philippe the hospitality of his house at Tide Mills but the king declined.

'Can I do anything more for your Majesty?' he asked.

'Oh! do get me a clean shirt', the king replied.

Catt was also a maltster. He was the sole owner of maltings at Newhaven and at Piddinghoe and, in partnership with the Vallance family, he also had an interest in Brighton's West Street Brewery and maltings at Kingston Buci, near Shoreham and Kemp Town.

When not making money this dedicated businessman devoted much of his time to growing fruit. In spite of the salt-laden air he managed to grow a fig tree at Tide Mills and his pear trees were grown in carefully-espaliered patterns on the walls of the mill buildings, here and there crossing windows as well as surrounding them.

In 1853 William Catt died leaving, for those days, an astounding £191,600, a sum that did not include any amount realised by the sale of the residual estate. Each of his nine surviving children received around £21,000.

Tidemills Project

In 2006 the Sussex Archaeological Society, in collaboration with the Sussex Probation service, started a long-term research project on the site. The project aims to make a full historical and archaeological survey of the mill and associated village, as well as the RNAS seaplane base and Chailey Heritage beach hospital. Volunteers are in the process of collating all documentary, cartographic, photographic and oral histories, in addition to on-site clearance/survey of the upstanding remains and excavation of buried deposits. It is hoped this will allow the development of the site through time to be understood and allow a fuller interpretation of the visible remains before further deterioration occurs.

The work has already uncovered much new information, including an early retaining wall on the old creek bank, and the building of a new timber quay, almost certainly by William Catt. Evidence of the development of Dale's racing stables in the 1920s and 30s and subsequent World War II military structures has also been uncovered.

One of the first armoured trains being tested on the Newhaven to Seaford line and, below, a seaplane at the base set up by the Admiralty at Tide Mills in the First World War.

4

The Railway Years

The arrival of the London, Brighton and South Coast Railway at Seaford in 1864 was the beginning of the end for the tidemill. Although it improved communications by giving the village its own station on the line from Newhaven, known as Bishopstone Beach Halt – a name that was changed to Tide Mills in the 1930s – farmers in the area were now finding it easier and cheaper to send their grain by rail to be milled at its destination rather than at source as hitherto.

In 1876 a violent storm breached the sea wall. Water poured over the shingle spit and across the village, destroying homes, flooding the fields and washing large amounts of shingle into the ponds. Considerable damage was done to the mill itself. Repairs were delayed because of a dispute with the Commissioners for Sewers over who was responsible for sea defences and by 1878, when George Catt repaired the sea wall, much of the south side of the ponds had been covered by shingle.

The inhabitants were used to coping with the ravages of the sea – and knew how to benefit from them. In 1785 upwards of 1,800 bushels of coal were swept away from the wharf near the mill and scattered all over the site. Very little was recovered and locally fires burned brightly in cottage hearths. Timbers, masts and spars recovered from wrecked ships marked boundary points, supported roofs and were used for a variety of other purposes all over the village. A cargo of tallow candles would provide free lighting for weeks and in 1887, when the Customs officers arrived to recover a crate of spirits they believed had been washed onto the beach from a wreck off the Isle of Wight, they found a lot of very merry villagers and nothing on the shore but shingle.

In 1879 the Newhaven Harbour Company bought Tide Mills from George's widow Emily for £11,000 and John Catt and Edgar Stoneham leased the mill from the harbour company and tried to keep it running. After four years the harbour company revoked the lease as it considered the site could more profitably be used for cement making. The windmill had been blown down during a gale, which had, at the same time, largely demolished the granary, and in May 1883 the corn-grinding machinery was offered for sale. The following year, as a consequence of the harbour company needing to complete the East Quay and build passenger facilities, the tidal flow up Mill Creek was restricted, thus denying barges access to the mill, although sluice gates still allowed tidal water to reach the village.

Negotiations with the Portland Cement Company about the use of Tide Mills collapsed in April 1884 as it had found a site better suited to its needs. The following year the harbour company decided to fill in the mill ponds with chalk brought by train from the site of Brighton College. Approval was given in 1890 for the mill buildings to be converted into a bonded warehouse which was leased to the Cafe Royal in Regent Street, then at the peak of its popularity as a meeting place for the literary and artistic lions of London society. Ten years later the restaurant terminated the lease and in 1901 much of the railway siding was removed and the mill and warehouse were demolished.

As work had begun to fall away the mill workers and their families left the village to seek jobs elsewhere and were replaced by railway employees and construction workers engaged on building Newhaven's new East Pier and sea defence walls. The Mill House changed hands a number of times but for some years was occupied by a Mrs Wilkes who had a large family of her own and often gave parties for the local children.

The rent of a four-roomed cottage in the village of Tide Mills at the beginning of the twentieth century was 2s 6d (12½p). There was no indoor sanitation – wet or fine, day or night, it was up the yard to the earth closet. Every drop of water required had to be carried in buckets from the outside water taps. There was a communal washhouse with a copper for boiling clothes, an outhouse containing a massive mangle, which made a tremendous din when the handle was turned, and a drying ground. Household rubbish had to be carried out to one of a number of large brick-lined pits and burned.

During World War One a giant sea-plane hangar was erected on the beach.

The Mill House still stood but most of the other mill buildings had gone and without the shelter they provided the cottages were very exposed to the weather. By the end of 1918 there were still families living in them without any modern conveniences, but one enterprising villager, Percy Thompson, did run a feed pipe from the communal outside pipe to inside his cottage. In the adjoining fields oxen continued to work but they were soon to be replaced by tractors. To make extra money one family set up a stall in the village and sold shellfish, sweets and lemonade to the visitors who each summer would take up residence in the beach huts and disused railway carriages that had appeared on the site.

In the 1920s part of the village was taken over by Captain David Dale's racing stables, which specialised in caring for horses that needed care and attention after an accident, perhaps, or too strenuous a racing season. The animals were exercised on sandy stretches of the shore and in the sea itself at low tide for Captain Dale believed, as had Dr Richard Russell before him, in the beneficial effects of sea bathing. It was on such an exercise outing that Clear Wind, owned by film magnate J Arthur Rank, reared up and fell backwards into the water. Although frantic efforts were made to save the animal from drowning they were not successful and to prevent it further distress a veterinary surgeon was summoned and it had to be shot.

The stables were again in the news in 1937, this time because Dorothy 'Dinkie' Dale, the captain's 18 year-old daughter, had left home after a family row when her father found out about her romance with his former head lad, 23 year-old Jack Sylvester – then a jockey riding for a trainer at Cheltenham. He refused to give his consent for them to marry so the couple applied to Cheltenham magistrates for permission and it was granted.

'Jack's a nice lad and we are both consenting to the wedding,' Mrs Dale told the *Daily Mirror*. 'We shall be sending them a wedding present.'

Another concern seeking a place to care for convalescents came to Tide Mills at about the same time. Chailey Heritage Craft School took over an Admiralty hut on the beach in 1924 and enlarged and converted it into an orthopaedic centre with a bungalow for attendant nurses beside it. Boys were sent there to convalesce after operations, and in the summer and at Christmas boarders from the craft school, who were not able to go home for a holiday, would come down for a change of scene at the seaside. The Chailey Heritage Marine Hospital at Tide Mills, to give it its full title, was formally opened by the Bishop of London, for it was in the chapter house of Southwark cathedral that the Guild of the Brave Poor Things, founded by Mrs Grace Kimmins, used to meet once a week in the 1890s.

These social meetings for the afflicted led to the founding of the first residential school with hospital treatment for the handicapped. It began with funds of a £5 note and seven boys from the Guild of the Brave Poor Things who were housed in an old workhouse at North Chailey. It was the aim of the founder to make every child, no matter how badly handicapped, either partially or wholly self-supporting. To this end they were each taught a craft – shoemaking and leatherwork, silver smithing and printing for the boys; needlework, dressmaking, toy making, weaving and laundry work for the girls.

Today Chailey Heritage is a nationally recognised non-maintained special school catering for seriously disabled children of all ages. Some 40 per cent of the pupils need residential care and this is provided in six purpose-built bungalows on the school site, together with twenty-four hour cover by care teams and nursing staff from the South Downs Health (NHS) Trust.

View towards the sea from the old level crossing gate.

View from the beach, looking towards Newhaven, of cottage ruins and mill buildings.

I

'Village life at Tide Mills' - English Heritage Interpretation board.

View, looking towards the sea, of an area thought to have been stables and a fruit garden.

View from beach of concrete ruins of 1930s Chailey children's hospital.

Ruins of the mill house.

III

Remains of boulder flint walls.

'Time line of Tide Mills' - English Heritage interpretation board.

Signpost of Vanguard Way, marking the walk from Croydon to Newhaven (c. 2007).

View of Tide Mills creek at half-tide.

Close view of creek showing sluice outlet.

Wider view of creek showing sluice outlet and the bridge.

VI

Close view of two sluice outlets and other remains.

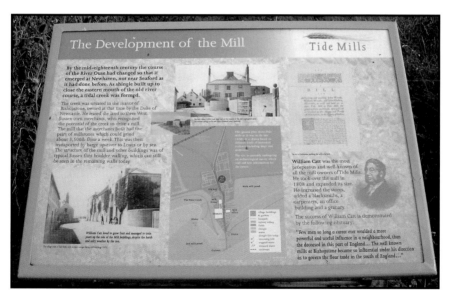

'The Development of the Mill' - English Heritage interpretation board.

Part of the concrete road adjacent to Tide Mills ruins.

View of ruins looking towards the sea from the old level crossing.

VIII

5

Tide Mills is Destroyed

In 1936 Seaford Urban District Council decided that because of the 'sanitary defects,' caused by the inhabitants emptying the contents of their earth closet receptacles on to the beach at low tide for the sea to deal with, about half the original cottages were unfit for human habitation. The area they occupied was declared a Clearance Area under the Housing Act of 1930. The same 'defects' must have applied to the holiday dwellings but they were not included in the order.

Chailey Heritage Craft School paid for a drainage scheme approved by the council to serve its marine hospital but the Southern Railway, which owned the cottages, was unable to secure approval for the scheme it put forward. The council seemed determined to condemn the cottages and destroy half the village.

By January 1939 the occupants had been re-housed and the sanitary inspector reported to the council that the work of demolishing buildings in the Tide Mills Clearance Area was in progress. Paradoxically, in March 1939 Seaford UDC extended for six months a licence for one of the beach huts known as Seaspray, although it stipulated that at the end of the extension period the hut must be removed.

The Second World War spelled the end of Tide Mills village. As the threat of German invasion grew, the Chailey Heritage children and the remaining civilian population were evacuated. In July 1940, to prepare for the defence of Newhaven Harbour, the army demolished all the buildings which would block the defenders' field of fire or provide shelter for any opposing troops who succeeded in getting ashore.

Tide Mills, Bishopstone, c. 1850. Reproduced with permission from the family of the artist, the late Stuart Broadhurst.

A pipeline was laid to Tide Mills from an enormous tank, sited in Bishopstone village, either for the purpose of emergency re-fuelling of ships or alternatively as a defence against invasion by pumping fuel oil into the sea and igniting it.

At the end of the war in 1945, Tide Mills was a ruined, bleak and deserted area.

In December 1993 an application by the Newhaven Society to have the area declared a village green was rejected by the environment committee of East Sussex County Council on the grounds that although the land had been used for informal recreation there was insufficient evidence to define it as required under the Commons Registration Act of 1965, neither had it been used 'as of right' exclusively by people from Newhaven, Seaford and South Heighton.

Currently, archaeological investigations are continuing on the Tide Mills site, which hopefully will reveal even more about the area.

BIBLIOGRAPHY

Banks, W. *Seaford Past and Present*. William Webb 1892

Bell, Martin. *Excavations at Bishopstone*. Sussex Archaeological Collections, vol 115. Sussex Archaeological Society, Lewes 1977

Elphick, George P. *Sussex Bells and Belfries*. Phillimore, Chichester 1970

Farrant J H. *The Evolution of Newhaven Harbour*. Sussex Archaeological Collections, vol 110. Sussex Archaeological Society, Lewes 1972

Farrant, Sue. *Bishopstone Tidemills*. Sussex Archaeological Collections, vol 113. Sussex Archaeological Society, Lewes 1975

Hackett, Kevin. *Tide Mills, the Development of a Village Round its Industry*. Unpublished dissertation.

McCarthy, Edna and 'Mac'. *Sussex River, Seaford to Newhaven*. Lindel Organisation, Seaford

Landon, M de. *Bishopstone Manor Through 900 Years*. Unpublished.

Lawrie, Rose Mary. *The Heritage Craft Schools, Chailey*. Article in Sussex County Magazine, pages 6-12. January 1951. T R Beckett, Eastbourne

Louis-Philippe at Newhaven. Unattributed article, Sussex County Magazine, pages 36-38, January 1937. T R Beckett, Eastbourne

Lucas, E V. *East Sussex Highways and Byways*. First pocket edition. Macmillan and Company, London 1924

Victoria County History of Sussex. Constable and Company, London

INDEX

S B Publications publish a wide range of Sussex guides and local history books. For information on other titles, please contact:

S B Publications
14 Bishopstone Road
Seaford
East Sussex
BN25 2UB

Website: *www.sbpublications.co.uk*